Brown University Athletics

From the Bruins to the Bears

Dedicated to my parents and my sister, whose belief in me and my abilities is unwavering, and to my two uncles and grandfathers who fostered my love of sports.

Brown University Athletics
From the Bruins to the Bears

Gordon M. Morton III

ARCADIA
PUBLISHING

ISBN 978-0-7385-1252-5

Published by Arcadia Publishing
Charleston, South Carolina

Printed in the United States of America

Library of Congress Control Number: 2003111339

For all general information, please contact Arcadia Publishing:
Telephone 843-853-2070
Fax 843-853-0044
E-mail sales@arcadiapublishing.com
For customer service and orders:
Toll-Free 1-888-313-2665

Visit us on the Internet at www.arcadiapublishing.com

Contents

ACKNOWLEDGMENTS

An undertaking of this magnitude does not happen without the help of many individuals. First and foremost, I must thank my family and friends for their constant support and encouragement from the beginning of this project. I am grateful to Amy Leavitt for her patience and understanding throughout this entire endeavor.

I am indebted to Chris Humm, Brown's sports information director, and Martha Mitchell, university archivist, for allowing me unfettered access throughout my research. Gayle Lynch and Ray Butti in the university archives were also extremely helpful with my many photographic requests.

The team at Arcadia Publishing has been a pleasure to work with, and I must thank publisher Amy Sutton and my editor, Tiffany Howe, who guided me through the entire production process. In addition, I am grateful for the careful eye and attention to detail of my contingent of proofreaders, particularly Bill Corrigan '58, Chris Humm, Beth James, Peter Mackie '59, and Lew Shaw '48.

I must recognize Provost Robert Zimmer, Yolanda Lamboy, and Michael Gaughan, who assisted me in securing the proper permission from Brown University for this work. I am grateful to Kevin Thompson for his legal counsel at the beginning of this project.

This book would have been incomplete without the help of photographers David Silverman and Tom Maguire, who graciously allowed me to reprint their images here. Their photographs are among the most captivating in the book and provide many of the shots in the final two chapters.

INTRODUCTION

While I have attempted to include some of the greatest athletes, successful athletic alumni, and the most compelling stories and moments in Brown history, it is impossible to include everyone and everything. Some were left out because I could not find a suitable photograph, while others were omitted because of space constraints. This book is merely a glimpse into the rich history and tradition of sports at the university.

I pored over thousands of photographs and selected what I feel are some of the best available images. I have also tried to represent each era in Brown's history. Obviously, some of the early photographs and statistics are difficult to collect, but I have included the best highlights from each period whenever possible. While it is difficult to compare athletes from different eras, I have tried to include those individuals who excelled during their time against the best competition available.

The bronze Bruno statue is shown here. The inscription on the base of the statue reads, "Given by alumni and undergraduates to Brown University to symbolize those qualities of strength, courage, endurance which go far to make men invincible." A ground-level plaque was installed in front of the bear in 1992, when the statue was moved from Marvel Gymnasium to the College Green. It describes the history of the statue: "The Brown Bear was originally cast in plaster by Eli Harvey. A fund-raising campaign to 'Put a Hair on the Bear' was led by Senator Theodore Francis Green, Class of 1887, and resulted in the commission of a bronze sculpture. In 1923, the bronze bear was dedicated at a ceremony on the campus during Commencement. For sixty-five years, the Bear stood in front of Marvel Gymnasium as a symbol of the strength, courage, and endurance of Brown University and her extended family. Now, here on the College Green, the Bear is re-dedicated to alma mater and to the men and women of Brown."

One

The Beginning of Intercollegiate Competition 1857–1900

While Harvard and Yale began intercollegiate competition in crew with a race in 1852, Brown was not far behind. In 1857, crew became the first organized intercollegiate sport at Brown, and on July 26, 1859, Brown raced against Harvard and Yale in a regatta on Lake Quinsigamond in Worcester, Massachusetts, becoming the third university in the country to compete in crew. The uniform of the Brown crew that day consisted of gray check pants, salmon silk shirts, and blue skullcaps. The Brown shell was called the *Atalanta* and was 44.5 feet long and weighed 150 pounds more than either the Harvard or Yale shells, causing Brown to finish third by a wide margin. Since this shell was too heavy, Brown tried a much lighter shell the following year. The 112-pound *Brunonia*, however, was not strong enough and broke up and sank in the middle of the race. The Brown crew figured everything out a few years later and defeated Harvard, Yale, and Amherst in a race in 1870.

Baseball became the second intercollegiate sport when Brown took on Harvard on June 27, 1863. The Brown contingent met the Harvard squad at the railroad station, took them to lunch, and gave them a tour of the library and laboratory before bringing them to the Dexter Training Ground for the game. Harvard defeated Brown in a game that lasted more than four hours and featured music from the American Brass Band.

Tennis began at Brown in the 1880s with the formation of the Brown University Lawn Tennis Association on April 14, 1883. During the late 1880s and early 1890s, the team enjoyed great success with stars Fred Hovey '90, Malcolm Chace '96, and Clarence Budlong '97. Hovey finished second in singles at the Intercollegiate Tennis Tournament in 1889 and went on to win six national titles after leaving Brown. Chace won in singles and doubles at the Intercollegiate Tennis Tournament in 1893, teaming with Budlong in doubles.

Ice hockey came to the United States in 1895, after a group of collegians, including several Brown men, brought the game back from Canada. A few years later, on January 19, 1898, Brown played Harvard at Franklin Field in Dorchester, Massachusetts, on a flooded baseball field. Brown brought seven players, which was considered the proper number at the time, and had no substitutes. Horace Day '01 scored the first goal, and Brown defeated Harvard 6-0. For many years, this was considered the first intercollegiate game in the country, although Yale and Johns Hopkins are reported to have played in 1896. The Brown-Harvard series is still the oldest continuing collegiate ice hockey rivalry in the country.

While the number of teams at Brown and the amount of intercollegiate competition were somewhat limited during this period, this would begin to change after the turn of the century.

The freshman class of 1873 crew defeated Harvard, Yale, and Amherst on July 22, 1870, on Lake Quinsigamond in Worcester, Massachusetts, securing Brown's first major intercollegiate victory. Shown, from left to right, are E.H. Luther, captain and bow; G.T. Brown, starboard stroke; F.A. Gower, stroke; A.M. Smith, port waist; A.D. McClellan, port bow; and W.E. Caldwell, starboard waist.

The class of 1874 crew never lost a race against the other Brown classes. On October 15, 1870, the freshman class of 1874 defeated the crews from the classes of 1871, 1872, and 1873. As sophomores on June 7, 1872, the class of 1874 again beat the other three classes. The race against the class of 1873 on October 1, 1872, was declared a draw. Notice that there were six rowers, instead of the typical four or eight rowers found today.

The 1878 football team is pictured here. Brown played its first intercollegiate football game at Amherst on November 12, 1878. Amherst won the contest four tries and one goal to nothing. The Brown team wore stiff, white canvas uniforms with brown hats and brown stockings, while Amherst wore more up-to-date jersey uniforms that allowed them to run more freely.

The 1879 baseball team won seven of its nine games, including two against Harvard, Amherst, and Trinity, and one against Yale. The squad lost only to Yale and Dartmouth. Upon the conclusion of the season, the team claimed the unofficial collegiate national championship, since the next best team, Yale, had won only 7 of its 11 games (a .636 winning percentage compared to Brown's .778 winning percentage).

J. Lee Richmond '80 pitched the first perfect game in professional baseball history, hurling a 1-0 victory for Worcester over Cleveland on June 12, 1880, just four days before his graduation. Richmond played for six years in the major leagues with Boston, Worcester, Providence, and Cincinnati. He had a 3.06 earned run average and 75 career victories, including 32 wins in 1880 and 25 victories in 1881. Richmond also amassed 262 career hits and batted .257.

The 1886 bicycle club is pictured here. The bicycle club was among the most popular student organizations during the 19th century.

The New England Intercollegiate Athletic Association held its first track-and-field meet on May 27, 1887, in Hartford, Connecticut. The members of the 1887 Brown team who competed are, from left to right, Charles Cooke '88, George Warren '89, John Williams '89, Eugene Perry '90, and Lucky Alonzo Lindsay '87. Cooke won the running broad jump, while Warren finished first in the pole vault.

The 1890 tennis team featured captain Fred Hovey '90 (seated on the grass on the right). Hovey won two national titles in singles and three national championships in doubles competition.

John Heisman attended Brown from 1887 to 1889 and went on to a successful 36-year coaching career. After retiring from coaching, he became physical director of the Downtown Athletic Club of New York. In his honor, the Downtown Athletic Club established the Heisman Trophy, which is presented annually to the outstanding collegiate football player in the nation.

The 1891 football team is shown on the steps of Lyman Gym. John Lindsey '92 (front row, second from the left) was the captain, manager, and coach of both the 1890 and 1891 teams and helped establish football at Brown on a permanent basis. The canvas jackets seen on several of the players were popular during this time because they were thought to make the players harder to tackle.

When Ned Weeks '93 arrived at Brown, he was accustomed to playing baseball barehanded. During his high school career, Weeks played shortstop, catcher, and first base without a glove. Through the winter of his freshman year at Brown, he continued to practice catching barehanded, but in the spring he was told that he could play first base at Brown only if he agreed to wear a glove. Weeks consented and helped revolutionize play at first base. During this era, first basemen played with their foot always on the bag, but Weeks became a pioneer by playing off the bag. His teammate, Fred Tenney '94, later introduced this style of play to the major leagues. In addition to his play at first, Weeks was a strong hitter and led the 1892 team with a .310 batting average and had 20 stolen bases. The speedy Weeks also ran track at Brown and was the New England champion in the 100-yard dash.

Dr. Frederick Marvel '94 captained the track team for two years and was the New England champion in the broad jump. He became Brown's first director of intercollegiate athletics in 1903 and held that post until 1938. His motto, "A team for every man and every man on a team," laid the groundwork for Brown's extensive programs of today. After his death (in 1938), the Brown Gymnasium was renamed in his honor.

Fencing at Brown began as an activity for the senior class in the 1890s, and the 1895 fencing team is pictured here. The team did not participate in intercollegiate competition until the early 1930s, when Fred Davis '35 organized and coached a team in December 1932.

During the Christmas vacation of 1894–1895, several collegians who had played the game of ice polo in the United States traveled to Canada to learn the game of ice hockey. The team played games in Montreal, Ottawa, Kingston, and Toronto. Each game consisted of two periods of ice hockey with seven men to a side, and two periods of ice polo with five men to a side. Each team won at its own game.

The 1897–1898 ice hockey team defeated Harvard 6-0 on January 19, 1898, in Brown's first intercollegiate game. The team went on to become intercollegiate champions after defeating Columbia and Yale in a series of games in New York City.

Edward North Robinson '96 was a third-team Walter Camp All-American in football and played on Brown's 1896 national championship baseball team. He served as the head football coach at Brown for 24 seasons and amassed 140 career victories.

The 1896 baseball team posted a 19-4 record against collegiate competition and won the national championship. The team defeated the University of Chicago, the Western Conference champion, in a best-of-three series. Chicago took the opener 1-0, but Brown rallied to win the next two games 13-3 and 6-5.

David Fultz '98 was a member of Brown's 1896 national championship baseball team. He was selected for the *Harper's* All-America baseball team in 1896 and 1897 and Walter Camp's All-America second team in football in 1897. Fultz went on to play three years of professional football and seven seasons in the major leagues. He posted a .271 lifetime batting average and had his best season in 1902, when he hit .302 and led the league with 109 runs.

The 1896 football team sported only a 4-5-1 record but had the richest manager in the country, John D. Rockefeller Jr. '97 (wearing the derby). Under his financial guidance, the football team was the first at Brown to finish the season with a profit.

John "Daff" Gammons '98 was an outfielder on the Brown baseball team that won the 1896 national championship. He played one year in the major leagues with the Boston Nationals and five seasons of professional football. Gammons returned to Brown as head football coach for three seasons, compiling a 17-10-2 record.

Willis Richardson '99 was a second-team Walter Camp All-American in 1898 and 1899. He kicked Brown's first field goal on November 6, 1898, and set Brown records with a 108-yard fumble return against Princeton and an 80-yard return of a blocked field goal against Colby. Richardson went on to play three seasons of professional football.

Two

The Introduction of the Bear 1901–1929

During the early 20th century, the bear became the mascot for Brown teams, and several more teams were established. Men's basketball debuted in 1901. The first practice was held on January 11, but because of a delay in the delivery of the baskets, the team could practice only passing and dribbling. Brown played its first intercollegiate basketball game on February 12, 1901, against Holy Cross in Worcester, Massachusetts. Brown fell 9-8 but avenged the loss four days later by defeating the Crusaders 29-10. The first part of the 20th century also saw the formation of lacrosse and soccer teams at Brown in 1926.

The Brown Bear was introduced to the university by Sen. Theodore Francis Green '87. Senator Green was on the building committee for Rockefeller Hall and was in charge of the furnishings for the new building.

"The central feature of the building was the trophy room and the central feature of that room was the great arch," Green wrote. "Here over the arch at the central point of student life at Brown, I put the head of a real brown bear, labeled beyond misinterpretation. The building was formally opened on January 20, 1904, so that is, I suppose, the Brown bear's birthday."

"From time to time, like a lot of other Brown men, I had felt the lack of a definite symbol of our college," Green explained. "I was annoyed at the painful attempts on the part of newspaper artists to provide us with one. Sometimes when a cartoon called for something to set up against the bulldog of Yale or the tiger of Princeton, a despairing artist would portray some colonial Puritan and let it go at that."

"So I set about selecting an appropriate symbol," Green said. "I wanted something alive, and though not human, such as we endow with humanlike qualities. First of all, I thought our symbol should be a mammal and one of fair size, so as to be capable of portrayal in the graphic and plastic arts impressively and without absurd exaggeration."

Green wanted a symbol that was indigenous to America and represented the qualities of Brown men: strength, independence, and courage. By process of elimination, he came up with the brown bear. He wrote that the brown bear "is truly American and, most important of all, it embodies and suggests those qualities we want to emphasize. While somewhat unsociable, it is good-natured and clean. While courageous and ready to fight, it does not look for trouble for its own sake, nor is it bloodthirsty. It is not one of a herd but acts independently. It is intelligent and capable of being educated (if caught young enough!) Remember, an athlete can make Phi Beta Kappa. Furthermore, the bear's color is brown; and its name is brown."

The symbol caught on quickly with the newspapers and the students, and a live bear first appeared at the Brown-Dartmouth football game on Saturday, November 25, 1905. The students obtained a bear named Dinks and a keeper for him, but on the day of the game, Dinks remained in the corner of his cage and would not move. All was not lost, however, as his mate, Helen, entertained the crowd and received a standing ovation.

While the bear remained the mascot, the use of Bruins as a nickname became more widespread by the 1930s.

David Hall '01 became the first Brown man to win an Olympic medal when he took home the bronze in the 800-meter race at the 1900 Olympics in Paris. During his collegiate career, Hall was a two-time New England champion in the mile and set a national half-mile record. In the trial heat at the Paris games, he established an Olympic mark of 1:56.2 in the 800-meter race on a grass track. In the finals, however, Hall finished third because of an unfortunate accident. He was a close second at the halfway mark, but the runner who ultimately finished second stepped on Hall's heel and tore off his right shoe. In the end, the winning time of 2:01.2 in the finals was far slower than Hall's record in the trials.

Tom Barry '03 was captain of the 1902 football team and a second-team Walter Camp All-American. He accounted for all of Brown's points against the University of Pennsylvania in 1902. Barry scored on runs of 50 and 31 yards and kicked a 28-yard field goal to help Brown beat Penn for the first time 15-6. He went on to coach at Tulane, Bowdoin, and Notre Dame, where he lost only one game in two years.

The senior class defeated the freshman class 16-2 to win the women's basketball college championship in 1903. The game turned a profit of $16.50 and was deemed a financial success.

Michael Lynch '04 pitched in the major leagues from 1904 through 1907, including three years with the Pittsburgh Pirates and one with the New York Giants. He compiled a 44-32 record with a 3.05 earned run average and two saves. He posted 53 complete games in 72 career starts. His best season came in 1905, when he went 17-9 with Pittsburgh.

The class of 1906 women's basketball team won the interclass championship as seniors.

Oscar Rackle '06 was the captain and coach of the 1905–1906 basketball team and led Brown in scoring for three years. When Brown defeated Dartmouth in 1905, Rackle scored 16 of Brown's 18 points.

The 1907 baseball team was undefeated against collegiate competition with a 16-0-1 record and won the national championship.

Don Pryor '08 set the single-game scoring record in basketball with 34 points, a mark that stood until 1938. It was an impressive feat considering that the games during this period were generally low scoring and teams rarely surpassed 30 points. Pryor served as captain and coach of the 1907–1908 basketball team and led the squad to an 11-8 record. He also coached the team during the 1908–1909 campaign.

The 1907 relay team went undefeated and featured William Prout '09 (second from the right). Prout went on to become captain of the U.S. track team and a member of the 400-meter relay team at the 1908 Olympics in London.

Wally Snell '13 was an All-American catcher as a senior. He played for the Boston Red Sox in 1913 and compiled a .375 batting average. He returned to Brown and was the head basketball coach, the head baseball coach, and an assistant football coach. During World War II, he served as Brown's director of athletics for four years.

The 1908 football team included captain Johnny Mayhew '09 (back row, second from the right), who was a first-team Walter Camp All-American in 1906 and a second-team Walter Camp All-American in 1908. Mayhew was also a member of the undefeated relay team of 1907 and captain of both the football and track teams as a senior. He set a world record of six seconds flat in the indoor 45-yard high hurdles.

Norm Taber '13 won the bronze medal in the 1,500-meter race at the 1912 Olympics in Stockholm. That year, he was also the New England champion in the mile. Taber broke the world record in the mile in 1915 with a 4:12.6 clocking. The previous record was established in 1886, and Taber's mark was not broken until 1923.

Arthur Bartlett '14 set Brown records in the hammer throw, the discus, and the shot put. He was the New England Intercollegiate Athletic Association champion in the shot put in 1911 and 1912 and broke the New England record as a sophomore. As a senior captain in 1914, Bartlett finished first in the discus at the New England meet.

Brown played in the 1916 Tournament of Roses football game against Washington State. The team of 21 players left Providence on Wednesday, December 22, and faced five days of railroad travel and six more days of preparation in California before the big game. The train arrived in Chicago on December 23 and stopped in Albuquerque on Christmas Day before arriving in Pasadena on Monday, December 27. While it is commonly believed to be the first Rose Bowl, Stanford actually played Michigan in 1902 (Michigan was leading 49-0 when Stanford gave up in the third quarter). Because of that lopsided score, the Tournament of Roses Association gave up football in favor of chariot races. The game returned to stay on January 1, 1916, when Brown battled Washington State on a rain-soaked and muddy field, before falling 14-0. Brown had two chances inside the 10-yard line but failed to score. After the game, the team departed for San Francisco and finally arrived back in Providence on January 7.

Wally Wade '17 was a guard on the Brown team that played in the Rose Bowl. He went on to a long and successful coaching career at Alabama, where he took three teams to the Rose Bowl, and at Duke, where he guided two teams to the Rose Bowl. Wade made the cover of *Time* on October 25, 1937, and the stadium at Duke was named in his honor in 1967.

William Earl Sprackling '12 (on the far left with the ball) was a three-time Walter Camp All-American, including a spot on Camp's first team in 1910. He threw the first touchdown pass in Brown history in 1908 and led Brown to its first victory over Yale in 1910, by accounting for 456 of the team's 608 yards.

Fritz Pollard '19 was the first African American to play in the Rose Bowl. After he helped Brown to an 8-1 mark in 1916, he became the first African American to make Walter Camp's All-America backfield. Pollard began his professional football career in 1919 with the Akron Pros of the American Professional Football Association, which became the National Football League (NFL) in 1922. He went on to star for the Milwaukee Badgers, the Hammond Pros of Indiana, and the Providence Steam Roller before finishing his career in 1926. He was the first African American head coach in the NFL and is enshrined in the college football Hall of Fame.

The 1919–1920 basketball team was led by captain Lou Pieri '20 (in the front row with the ball). He helped revive basketball at Brown after a six-year hiatus and coached and captained the 1918–1919 squad after convincing the university to grant varsity status to the basketball program. He went on to become owner of the Rhode Island Auditorium and the Providence Reds hockey team. In 1949, he became part owner of the Boston Celtics.

Josh Weeks '19 started at right end for the football team as a freshman when Brown played in the Rose Bowl on January 1, 1916. He served as captain of the 1918 football team and earned a spot on Walter Camp's All-America second team that year.

Zenas Bliss '18 (second from the left) was the navigator on the last two J-boats to defend the America's Cup, *Rainbow* and *Ranger*. After losing the first two races in 1934 to England's *Endeavor*, *Rainbow* came back to win four straight. *Ranger* won 32 of 34 trial races and then defeated *Endeavor II* in four straight races to win the America's Cup in 1937. Bliss was an engineering professor, dean, and provost at Brown.

Davy Jones '24 was a three-time Intercollegiate Swimming Association national champion in the 100-yard dash, and a three-time All-American. In more than 40 intercollegiate races in the 100-yard dash, Jones was never beaten. A two-time captain of the Brown team, he set the national 100-yard record.

The class of 1923 junior team won the women's basketball interclass championship. The team included, from left to right, Frances Wright (captain), Dorothy Patton, Joanna Shea, Janet Chew, Eleanor Parmelee, and Ruth Preston.

Jack Keefer '25 was selected to Walter Camp's All-America third team as a senior. He later played professional football with the Providence Steam Roller and the Dayton Triangles of the NFL.

Mian "Mike" Gulian '23 was the captain of the 1922 football team, which went 6-2-1 and posted four shutouts. He was selected by Walter Camp to his All-America third team and went on to play three years of professional football.

Hal Neubauer '25 played football, baseball, and tennis at Brown. He pitched for the Boston Red Sox during the 1925 season and posted a perfect 1-0 record in seven relief appearances.

The 1926 lacrosse team was Brown's first organized lacrosse team. They compiled a 1-3-1 record, including a win against Dartmouth and a tie versus the Yale junior varsity. The team fell twice to the Boston Lacrosse Club and once to Harvard. Lacrosse continued at Brown until 1937 and was revived again in the early 1960s.

John Spellman '24 won a gold medal at the 1924 Olympics in Paris. He won six of seven bouts to capture the light-heavyweight championship. When he competed in the U.S. Olympic Trials, he was penalized by the dean's office for taking time off from classes. Spellman was the captain of both the football and wrestling teams at Brown and went undefeated in wrestling in 1924. He went on to play eight seasons of professional football.

Frank "Dick" Spellman '28 was a two-time New England champion and captain of the wrestling team. He posted a 17-3-1 overall record at Brown. While wrestling at 158 pounds during his sophomore year, Spellman compiled a 6-2 record and won the New England championship. He went undefeated as a junior, with a 7-0-1 mark, and again won the New England crown. During his senior year, Spellman went 4-1 and finished second at the New England championship.

Brown Field was dedicated twice during the 1925 football season. The program from the first dedication against Yale is shown here. The second dedication against Harvard was also significant because it marked the first time the Crimson had ever played football at Brown in more than 30 meetings between the schools. Brown played all 10 of its games at home in 1925, the first in the new $350,000 stadium.

The 1926 football team became known as the "Iron Men" after the 11 starters played all 60 minutes without substitution in consecutive weeks against Yale and Dartmouth and well into the fourth quarter against Harvard later in the season. They compiled a 9-0-1 record and outscored their opponents 223-36. However, they lost their chance for an undefeated and untied season when Colgate earned a 10-10 deadlock in the final game of the season.

Orland Smith '27, one of the Iron Men, was an offensive guard and defensive tackle on the undefeated 1926 football team. Smith was selected by Grantland Rice as a first-team All-American, and the Associated Press named him a third-team All-American. After graduating, he played on the 1928 Providence Steam Roller, which won the NFL championship.

Dave Mishel '27 was an Associated Press honorable mention All-American as a senior. He led the undefeated Iron Men of 1926 in scoring with 51 points on four touchdowns, 18 conversions, and three field goals. In Brown's 7-0 upset of Yale in 1926, Mishel was the key to Brown's victory, as he completed five of nine passes, threw the touchdown pass to Red Randall, and kicked the extra point.

Bill Quill '27 pitched 18 innings against Providence College on May 22, 1926. The Friars jumped out to an early lead with four runs in the second inning and one in the third and appeared to be in control of the game. Providence's four runs in the second came on three hits, one sacrifice, and three Brown errors. However, Brown rallied and came back with a run in the fourth and another in the fifth and tied the game with three runs in the seventh. The teams remained deadlocked for 11 innings with five runs each. In the 18th inning, with the bases loaded and two outs, the Friars scored the winning run and captured a 6-5 victory. The game began at 3:00 p.m. and did not end until 7:35 p.m., but most of the 5,500 fans stayed until the end. Quill finished with five strikeouts and five walks. Brown had 13 hits to Providence's 11, but Brown stranded 19 men on base while the Friars left 12.

Albert Cornsweet '29 was a two-time Associated Press honorable mention All-American in football and went on to play professionally. He was a three-time New England Intercollegiate wrestling champion and was the runner-up in the national open wrestling championship. He compiled a 19-1 dual-meet record and a set a Brown record with a .950 career winning percentage. Cornsweet was also an All-American in lacrosse and played professionally for one year.

Harry Cornsweet '29 lost only one match in his wrestling career at Brown. As a sophomore, he posted a 7-1 record in the unlimited division, with his only defeat coming on a split overtime decision. He won his first New England championship that season. Cornsweet went 5-0 as a junior and 7-0 as a senior, and he won New England crowns both seasons. He posted a 19-1 career record and set the Brown record with a .950 career winning percentage.

John Collier '29 won the bronze medal in the 110-meter high hurdles at the 1928 Olympics in Amsterdam. As a senior at Brown, he was the indoor and outdoor Intercollegiate Association of Amateur Athletics of America (IC4A) champion in the high hurdles. Collier came out of retirement in 1934 and broke the world record in the 60-yard high hurdles.

Roy "Red" Randall '28 was the quarterback of the undefeated Iron Men of 1926 and was an Associated Press honorable mention All-American. He served as captain of the 1927 team and set a Brown record with a 74-yard punt return.

While still a freshman at Brown, Roland MacKenzie '29 was named to the 1926 U.S. Walker Cup team with golfing legends Bobby Jones, Francis Ouimet, and Jess Sweetser. MacKenzie played on the Walker Cup team with Bobby Jones three times and posted a 5-1 record. He also qualified for the U.S. National Amateur Golf Championship five times and advanced to the semifinals in 1927. At the 1925 nationals at Oakmont, MacKenzie won the qualifying medal with a score of 145 and Jones shot a 147. MacKenzie had his best showing at the 1927 nationals when he advanced to the semifinals before losing a 37-hole battle with Chick Evans.

Three

The Dropping and Reestablishment of Teams 1930–1953

The 1930s, 1940s, and early 1950s were a tumultuous time for many athletic teams at Brown. While the country was in the midst of the Depression and World War II, several Brown teams were discontinued. Many, however, were reestablished a few years later. The war had an effect on men's basketball, whose schedule changed dramatically from 1942 through 1945 with competition against several military teams. Wrestling was discontinued after the 1939–1940 season and revived in 1946. Fencing faced a similar fate when it was abandoned in 1943 and resumed in 1946.

Men's ice hockey did not field a varsity team from the 1939–1940 season through the 1946–1947 season because of financial concerns. Some informal teams, however, were organized and coached by Frank Mazzeo, the campus barber. In 1946, the team was not permitted to play under the college name, so they called themselves the "Providence Clippers." Hockey became an officially recognized sport again during the 1947–1948 season, and former star player W.E.S. Moulton '31 returned to coach the team. Just three seasons later, Moulton guided the 1950–1951 squad to the Pentagonal League title and a second-place finish in the NCAA tournament.

Lacrosse was dropped in 1937 but returned in 1949 with an informal team named the Narragansett Lacrosse Club. The team continued informally until 1961, when it was recognized by the administration as a club sport. After two successful seasons, the team gained varsity status in 1963. The squad posted a winning record in each of its first 14 seasons and won the Ivy title in 1969.

Crew was given up in favor of baseball in 1886 due to the difficulty in raising funds for both sports. It remained dormant until Harlan Bartlett '51 and Jim Donaldson '51 got together to revive the sport at Brown. Both men had rowed in prep school, and in the fall of 1948, they borrowed Mr. and Mrs. Bartlett's Oldsmobile and drove to Donaldson's alma mater, St. Andrew's School in Middletown, Delaware, where they purchased a used eight-oared shell for $100. The shell was rumored to be at least 30 years old and had once belonged to Harvard. They transported the 65-foot shell 450 miles back to Providence on the top of the 17-foot Oldsmobile, and stored it at the Narragansett Boat Club. Harvard and Princeton donated some old oars to the fledgling crew, and Robert Read agreed to serve as a volunteer coach. Crew was an informal sport in the spring of 1949, and in the second informal season in 1950, the team was allowed to use the name "Brown University Rowing Association, an Informal Organization of Brown Undergraduates." This recognition permitted the team to enter intercollegiate competition, and in the first race, Brown defeated Clark University by four lengths and threw coxswain Ralph Gerstle '51 into the Seekonk River to celebrate the victory. The team continued informally until 1961, when crew was recognized as a varsity sport and Vic Michalson became the program's first full-time coach.

There was a greater sense of stability at the end of this period, as many of the Brown teams were now more firmly established at the university.

Joseph Buonanno '34 was a two-time Associated Press honorable mention All-American in football and captain of the 1933 team. An excellent pole vaulter, he won the New England Intercollegiate title three times and competed in the U.S. Olympic Trials.

Archery was a popular women's sport in the 1930s, and the 1932 team is shown here. The team would hold telegraphic tournaments against other colleges in which each school competed at home and telegraphed the results to the other school.

Tom Gilbane '33 was an All-East selection in football in 1932 and was the starting center in the East-West game. He served as captain of the track team and won the IC4A championship in the shot put.

The 1932 football team, led by captain Bill Gilbane '33 (back row, second from the left), won its first seven games before falling to Colgate on Thanksgiving morning. Gilbane earned All-East honors and played in the North-South game. He also played baseball, won the New England freshman wrestling championship, and was the boxing champion at Brown.

Paul Mackesey '32 was the captain of the 1931 football team, which went 7-3. He was a two-time Associated Press honorable mention All-American and went on to play professional football. Mackesey served as the director of athletics at Brown from 1947 through 1962.

The 1930–1931 hockey team included W.E.S. "Wecky" Moulton '31 (front row, fifth from the left). Moulton was Brown's first hockey All-American and was selected by the *Boston Post* as the Outstanding Hockey Player in New England in 1931. He returned to Brown as a coach and led the hockey team to consecutive Pentagonal League crowns in 1950 and 1951 and a second-place finish at the 1951 NCAA championship.

Albina Osipowich '33 won two gold medals at the 1928 Olympics in Amsterdam. She finished first in the 100-meter freestyle in a new world record time of 1:11 and won a second gold medal as a member of the U.S. 4x100-meter relay team.

The 1933 soccer team included Amby Murray '36 (front row, fourth from the right) and goalie Henry Tolman '35 (back row, center, with "Brown" across his chest). Murray graduated as Brown's leading scorer with 27 goals and 10 assists for 64 points. Tolman posted three shutouts in Brown's six games in 1933 and led the team to a 3-2-1 record and its first winning season. He earned first-team All-America recognition in both 1933 and 1934.

Jean Bauer '33 was a two-time medalist at the USGA National Amateur Championship (1935 and 1941) and a three-time Rhode Island state golf champion (1940, 1941, and 1942). As an undergraduate, she was a two-time captain of the basketball team and competed in archery, baseball, bowling, field hockey, fist ball, swimming, and tennis. Additionally, she became the first sophomore to win the Pembroke Blazer. Bauer won the Augusta Southern Nationals in 1934, the Miami-Biltmore Doherty Cup and the Mason-Dixon Championship in 1935, the New England title in 1937, and the Southwest Championship in 1939. She won the medal round and set a tournament record with a score of 79 at the 39th Annual Women's Golf Championship in Minneapolis in 1939, bettering the old mark by three strokes. Bauer also set a women's record at Wannamoisett Country Club in 1935 with a score of 75.

Franklin White '33 was a three-time New England champion in the 150-yard backstroke and a three-time All-American. He finished fifth in the 150-yard backstroke at both the 1931 and 1933 national championships.

The 1934 baseball team featured Charlie Butler '36 (the tall player in the back row) and Amby Murray '36 (middle row, third from the left). Butler was a hard-hitting first baseman who left Brown with seven career batting marks, including a .328 batting average. Murray was a southpaw who compiled a 7-3 record as a senior and graduated with the Brown records for complete games, innings pitched, strikeouts, and victories. He went on to pitch one year in the major leagues with the Boston Braves.

John McLaughry '40 was a three-time Associated Press honorable mention All-American and the captain of the 1939 football team coached by his father, Tuss McLaughry. He played in the East-West Shrine game and was the captain of the College All-Stars when they defeated the New York Giants. He later played professional football for the Giants and went on to a successful coaching career at Union, Amherst, and Brown.

The 1936 men's soccer team was led by William Margeson '37 (front row, last player on the right). The team went undefeated with a 7-0-3 record and captured the New England Intercollegiate Soccer Association title. Margeson led the league in scoring with 12 goals, including hat tricks against Yale, Clark, and Tufts. He finished his career with 20 goals and nine assists for 49 points, the second highest total at Brown at that time.

One of the most versatile athletes in Brown history, Ernie Savignano '42 competed in football, basketball, hockey, baseball, and track. He was an Associated Press honorable mention All-American in football in 1940 and was the captain of the 1941 football team. He later coached at Brown and worked as an assistant athletic director.

The 1938–1939 men's basketball team posted a 16-4 record, won the New England championship, and played Villanova in the first NCAA tournament. One of only eight teams in the inaugural tournament, Brown did not shoot well in the first half and fell to Villanova 42-30. A year earlier in February 1938, Harry Platt '40 (front row, wearing No. 21) set the Brown record for points in a game with 48 against Northeastern.

Tommy Nash '40 was an All-East end in football and played for the College All-Stars in their victory over the New York Giants. Nash was also a member of the baseball and wrestling teams. As a freshman, he was undefeated in wrestling and won the New England Intercollegiate title.

Irving "Shine" Hall '39 was an Associated Press honorable mention All-American in 1937 and 1938. On Thanksgiving morning in 1938, he scored 27 points to lead Brown to a 36-27 victory over Columbia and its star, Sid Luckman.

Henry "Bob" Margarita '44 set the Brown single-game rushing record with 233 yards against Columbia in 1942. A two-time Associated Press honorable mention All-American, he went on to play for the Chicago Bears. He led the Bears in rushing and was third in the league in 1944. He led the team in rushing again in 1945, finishing fourth in the league and earning All-Pro honors in the backfield with Sammy Baugh, Bob Waterfield, and Steve Van Buren.

The 1936–1937 men's ice hockey team featured goalie Jack Skillings '37 (front row, sixth from the left), who set a Brown record with 76 saves in a game against Harvard on December 20, 1935. Skillings went on to play with the Hershey Bears of the Eastern Hockey League during the 1937–1938 season.

Carl Paulson '46 became Brown's first individual NCAA champion when he won the 200-yard breaststroke in 1944. He earned All-America honors in 1943 and 1944. Paulson was also a three-time New England champion in the 200-yard breaststroke and the 300-yard individual medley.

The 1940 baseball team included Walt Jusczyk '41 (front row, fifth from the right, with a bat). One of Brown's greatest hurlers, Jusczyk set the Brown career records for strikeouts, victories, shutouts, complete games, and innings pitched. He was signed by the Brooklyn Dodgers, but his career was interrupted by World War II.

George Menard '50 was a first-team All-Pentagonal League choice in 1949 and was the captain of the 1950 squad, which won Brown's first Pentagonal League championship. Menard was also an outstanding catcher on the baseball team and was signed by the New York Yankees.

The 1946–1947 basketball team was led by captain George "Woody" Grimshaw '47 (front row, with the ball) and head coach Weeb Ewbank (front row, on the right). Grimshaw became the first Brown man to score 1,000 points in a career. He was also an Associated Press honorable mention All-American in football in 1946. Ewbank was the head basketball coach for only one season and went on to coach the New York Jets to victory in Super Bowl III.

Bob Bennett '49 won the bronze medal in the hammer throw at the 1948 Olympics in London. He set Brown records in the hammer and the 35-pound weight and was the IC4A champion in both events.

Don Colo '50 never played football before coming to Brown, but he became a successful defensive lineman in the NFL. He played nine seasons of professional football, including six with the Cleveland Browns, and was a three-time All-Pro. Colo was a captain and defensive right tackle for the Browns when they won the world championship under legendary coach Paul Brown.

Frank "Moe" Mahoney '50 had offers from the Boston Celtics, the Philadelphia Eagles, and the Chicago White Sox after graduation and played two years with the Celtics. Mahoney served as captain of the basketball team at Brown and scored 828 career points. He also set a Brown record in football with seven receptions against Princeton in 1949.

Gil Borjeson '51 was captain of the track team and the New England and IC4A shot put champion. As a senior, he was the IC4A and NCAA hammer throw champion, and he qualified for the 1952 U.S. Olympic Trials, where he finished fourth.

Dick Phillips '50 was the national indoor and outdoor champion in the high jump during the 1948–1949 season. He also won the high jump at the Indoor and Outdoor Heptagonal Championships in 1949 and 1950. His top leap of six feet eight inches came at the 1949 Indoor Heptagonal Championship when he set a meet record.

Joe Paterno '50 was a quarterback and defensive back and graduated with the school record for interceptions. In his final game at Brown, on Thanksgiving morning in 1949, Brown trailed Colgate 26-7 with 17 minutes left but rallied to crush Colgate 41-26 behind the running and passing of Paterno. He also made a key interception late in the game to seal the victory. The 1949 team, with Paterno serving as captain, finished the season with an 8-1 record, outscoring its opponents 263-94. After graduation, he was accepted at Boston University Law School but was persuaded by his college coach, Rip Engle, to follow him to Penn State to become an assistant coach. When Engle retired, Paterno became the head coach in 1966. He became one of the most successful coaches in college football history. In October 2001, he broke Bear Bryant's record of 323 wins to become the winningest Division I-A college football coach. Under Paterno, Penn State had five undefeated teams from 1968 to 1994 and won national titles in 1982 and 1986.

Don Sennott '52 set the Brown hockey record with 159 career points. He also set the game, season, and career marks for assists, with many of those passes going to linemate Bobby Wheeler '52. Sennott was a first-team All-Pentagonal League honoree in 1951 and 1952.

Don Whiston '51 was a first-team All-American and the Most Outstanding Player of the 1951 NCAA Ice Hockey Championship. He was a first-team All-Pentagonal League selection in 1950 and 1951 and helped Brown to Pentagonal League titles in both seasons. Whiston was a goalie on the U.S. hockey team that won the silver medal at the 1952 Olympics in Oslo.

Bobby Wheeler '52 was a first-team All-America selection and the Most Valuable Player in the Pentagonal League in 1952. He graduated with the records for most goals in a game, season, and career. Against Springfield on January 31, 1952, he scored eight goals to lead Brown to a 22-2 victory. He also set Brown records with 12 career game-winning goals and 10 career hat tricks.

One of the greatest wrestlers in Brown history, J. Dana Eastham '53 lost only one dual-meet match during his varsity career and graduated with the highest career winning percentage. Eastham finished second in his weight class at the 1952 Olympic Trials.

Angus MacLean '53 won 34 of 36 matches during his four years on College Hill. Wrestling at 137 pounds, he posted a perfect 10-0 record during his freshman year. He had an 8-1 record as a sophomore and a perfect 9-0 mark as a junior. MacLean was a co-captain of the 1952–1953 team and compiled a 7-1 record.

Four

The Formation of the Ivy League 1954–1970

The terms "Ivy colleges" and "Ivy League" first appeared in print during the 1930s. Prior to the formalization of any league, several sportswriters, including Stanley Woodward and Caswell Adams of the *New York Herald Tribune*, used the phrase to describe the athletic teams of some of the oldest schools in the East.

In February 1935, Associated Press sports editor Alan Gould wrote, "The so called 'Ivy League' which is in the process of formation among a group of the older Eastern universities now seems to have welcomed Brown into the fold and automatically assumed the proportions of a 'big eight.' "

In January 1936, however, the *Brown Daily Herald* reported that "plans to make the 'Ivy League' official, as far as football is concerned, have been abandoned for the time being." The story went on to say that "Army and one other college have declined to make it a 'big ten.' "

The league did not form for another 10 years until the first Ivy Group Agreement was signed in November 1945. The agreement applied only to football and addressed common tenets and practices regarding academic standards, eligibility requirements, and need-based financial aid, but it did not address scheduling. Teams were not obligated to play each other, and for several years, Brown did not play Cornell, Dartmouth, or the University of Pennsylvania in football.

While the first agreement covered only football, it was extended in February 1954 to include all intercollegiate sports. The agreement stated, "The Group affirm their conviction that under proper conditions, intercollegiate competition in organized athletics offers desirable development and recreation for players and a healthy focus of collegiate loyalty. These conditions require that the players be truly representative of the student body and not composed of a group of specially recruited athletes. . . . In the total life of the campus emphasis upon intercollegiate competition must be kept in harmony with the essential educational purposes of the institution." While the agreement was signed in 1954, official Ivy League competition did not begin until the 1956–1957 season.

Although Brown struggled against its Ivy brethren in most sports, the Bruins dominated in men's soccer. Brown won six consecutive Ivy titles from 1963 through 1968, amassing a record of 36-3-3 against Ivy competition.

The men's ice hockey team was also successful during this period, finishing first or second in the Ivy League for five consecutive seasons from 1962–1963 through 1966–1967. The team posted a 33-15-2 mark over that span and captured the Ivy championship during the 1964–1965 campaign.

Lou Murgo '54 became only the second Brown man to surpass 1,000 points and graduated as the basketball career scoring leader. Murgo also played baseball at Brown and was the captain of both the basketball and baseball teams. After his graduation from Brown, he signed a professional baseball contract with the Baltimore Orioles and played for two years in their farm system.

Gerry Alaimo '58 left Brown as the third leading scorer and second leading rebounder in school history. He once scored 38 points and had 21 rebounds in a game against Penn in 1956. Alaimo pulled down 26 rebounds in his final game to lead Brown to a 76-67 victory over the University of Rhode Island. He went on to coach the Bruins for nine seasons and guided the 1973–1974 squad to a school-record 17 wins.

Ed Tooley '55 set the Brown single-game record with 32 rebounds against Northeastern. He placed 11th nationally with 436 rebounds during the 1954–1955 season. Tooley also set Brown records for rebounds in a season and a career. He scored a career-high 39 points against Amherst in 1954, the second-best single-game performance in school history at the time.

Kay Cashman '56 and Eleanor Brown '57 are shown bowling in Sayles Gymnasium during the mid-1950s.

Paul Choquette Jr. '60 was an Associated Press honorable mention All-American and a first-team All-Ivy selection in 1958 and 1959. He graduated as Brown's career rushing leader with 1,555 yards. Choquette led Brown in rushing in each of his three seasons. During both his junior and senior years, he was ranked among the top 10 rushers in the nation.

Quarterback Frank Finney '59 won the George Bulger Lowe Award as the Outstanding Player in New England and was an Associated Press honorable mention All-American. As a senior in 1958, he led the Ivy League in passing, scoring, and total offense and was a first-team All-Ivy pick.

Ted Turner '60 was captain of the Brown sailing team and commodore of the Brown Yacht Club. He was the skipper of *Courageous*, which defeated *Australia* 4-0 to win the 1977 America's Cup. Turner was named the U.S. Sailing Yachtsman of the Year in 1970, 1973, 1977, and 1979.

Robert Lowe '61 was a two-time Outdoor Heptagonal champion in the two-mile run and set a new Brown and Heptagonal record with a 9:05.8 clocking in 1961. He also set an IC4A meet record in the three-mile run and won the IC4A steeplechase in 1961. As a senior, Lowe finished first at the New England, Heptagonal, and IC4A cross country championships.

Tom Draper '64 set Brown lacrosse records with 123 career goals and 162 career points. He was an All-Ivy, All-New England, and All-America pick as a senior in 1964.

Joe Tebo '58 (No. 24) became the first Brown basketball player to earn first-team All-Ivy honors. He finished his career with 1,319 points, then a Brown record. Tebo scored 41 points against Cornell in 1957 to lead Brown to an 88-56 victory.

Alan Young '64 was a first-team All-Ivy pick as a senior and graduated as the career scoring leader with 32 goals and 11 assists for 75 points. Against the University of Connecticut in 1963, he tied the Brown record for goals in a game with 5 and set the mark for points in a game with 11.

The 1963 men's soccer team posted an 11-2-1 record, including a 6-1 mark in Ivy play, to capture Brown's first Ivy title in men's soccer. The team also reached the NCAA tournament for the first time in Brown soccer history and advanced to the quarterfinals before falling to Army.

Dave Farley '64 won the IC4A indoor mile in 4:13.7 as a junior and won the IC4A outdoor mile as a senior with a time of 4:06.6. He also captured the Outdoor Heptagonal Championship in the 880-yard run in 1964.

Mike Cingiser '62 was the first Brown basketball player to be named first-team All-Ivy for three consecutive seasons. With two games remaining in his career, Cingiser was 43 points shy of the Brown career scoring mark. He poured in 28 points against Dartmouth and finished with 27 points against the University of Rhode Island to set a new Brown record with 1,331 career points. Cingiser returned to coach at Brown in 1981 and led the Bruins to the Ivy title and an NCAA tournament appearance in 1986.

Leon Bryant '65 became the first Brown hockey player to be named first-team All-Ivy in each of his three varsity seasons. He finished his career with 55 goals and 75 assists for 130 points, the third highest total at that time.

Don Carcieri '65 played football and baseball at Brown. He earned three varsity letters in football, playing quarterback as a sophomore and junior before switching to defensive back as a senior. As a quarterback in 1962 and 1963, he completed 14 of 36 passes for 171 yards. He also pitched for the Brown nine. Carcieri was elected governor of Rhode Island in 2002.

Bob Gaudreau '66 was a two-time first-team All-American and a three-time first-team All-Ivy selection. He won the Walter Brown Trophy in 1965 as the Outstanding Player in the East and took home the Leonard Fowle Award in 1966 as the Most Valuable Player in the East. He was voted the Outstanding Defenseman in New England in 1966 and played on the 1968 U.S. Olympic hockey team.

Terry Chapman '65 was a two-time first-team All-Ivy choice and the captain of Brown's 1964–1965 team, which won the Ivy title and played in the NCAA tournament. He ended his career with 67 goals, the third-best total in Brown history at the time. His 127 career points ranked fourth all-time when he graduated.

Quarterback Bob Hall '66 won the 1965 George Bulger Lowe Award as the top football player in New England. He was an Associated Press honorable mention All-American and first-team All-Ivy pick. As a senior in 1965, he ranked in the top 10 nationally in passing and total offense. Hall graduated with 15 Brown records and five Ivy marks.

John Parry '65 was a two-time first-team All-Ivy choice and a two-time Associated Press honorable mention All-American. He set five Brown and six Ivy League records. As a junior in 1963, Parry was 12th in the nation in pass receiving. He went on to become the director of athletics at Brown from 1979 through 1990.

Wayne Small '68 was a first-team All-American and a two-time first-team All-Ivy pick. His 68 career goals and 76 career assists were the second highest totals in Brown history at the time. He also set the Brown record for hat tricks in a season with six in his senior year.

George Armiger '67 was a first-team All-American in lacrosse as a junior in 1966 and also earned a spot on the All-America team as a senior in 1967. He was a two-time first-team All-Ivy selection and played in the North-South game.

Richard Alter '66 (left) and William Carr '66 (right) were co-captains of the 1966 lacrosse team. Alter was an All-Ivy, All-New England, and All-America selection in 1966 and was named the Outstanding Lacrosse Player of 1966 by the U.S. Intercollegiate Lacrosse Association (USILA). He graduated with the records for most saves in a game, a season, and a career. Carr left Brown second all-time in scoring with 123 points. He was a two-time first-team All-Ivy pick and earned All-America honors as a senior.

In the early days of women's ice hockey at Brown in the 1960s, the team had to raise its own funds. One of the more interesting fundraisers was a game between the women's team and the men's junior varsity, who played with brooms.

Pat Migliore '68 was an All-American center back on three of the great Brown soccer teams of the mid-1960s. As a senior in 1967, he led a defense that surrendered only nine goals in 14 games. His teams captured three Ivy League championships and were unbeaten in Ivy play with a 20-0-1 mark. Overall, Migliore's teams posted a 36-2-2 record and outscored their opponents 141-34.

Vic DeJong '68 set the Brown soccer records for assists in a season and a career. The All-Ivy and All-American forward was the playmaker for the Brown offense that scored 47 goals in 14 games in 1967. A year earlier, Brown tallied an even more impressive 49 goals in 12 games. DeJong's teams won three consecutive Ivy titles and went undefeated against Ivy League competition. During his three varsity seasons, Brown compiled a 36-2-2 overall mark and outscored its opponents 141-34.

Coach Vic Michalson is shown with the 1969 crew captain, Dick Dreissigacker '69. Michalson was Brown's first full-time crew coach and led Brown to its first Ivy title in 1972 and its first Intercollegiate Rowing Association (IRA) title in 1979. Dreissigacker was a member of the 1970 U.S. national team heavyweight eight and the 1971 U.S. national team heavyweight four. He rowed in the 1972 Olympics in the U.S. coxless four and later developed the rowing oar that became the standard for college crews.

Rick Landau '68 (left) and Bill Reynolds '68 (right), shown here with coach Stan Ward, were the co-captains of the 1967–1968 basketball team. Landau and Reynolds each finished with a .795 career free throw percentage, tying each other for the Brown record. Reynolds also amassed 909 career points, the seventh highest total at the time. Landau went on to a successful career on Wall Street, while Reynolds became a sports columnist for the *Providence Journal* and authored several books.

Curt Bennett '70 was a first-team All-New England, All-East, and All-America selection in 1970 and a two-time first-team All-Ivy pick. While still a sophomore at Brown in 1968, Bennett was drafted 16th overall by the St. Louis Blues, but he did not turn pro until 1970. He played for 10 years in the NHL with the New York Rangers, Atlanta Flames, and St. Louis Blues and appeared in two All-Star games. He finished his NHL career with 152 goals and 182 assists.

A first-team All-Ivy and second-team All-America pick in 1968 and 1969, Herman Ssebazza '70 (No. 9, with the ball) helped lead the Bruins to the Ivy League title and the NCAA Final Four in 1968. Before he arrived at Brown, Ssebazza played on the Ugandan national team in 1966.

Five

THE GROWTH OF WOMEN'S SPORTS 1971–1989

After Brown and Pembroke merged in July 1971, athletic opportunities for women increased dramatically. In December 1971, with women enrolled as undergraduates in all eight Ivy institutions, the presidents unanimously approved a proposal that "the Ivy Group rules of eligibility shall not be construed to discriminate on grounds of sex." League championships in women's sports began in May 1974 with the first official Ivy championship in women's crew.

The women's outdoor track team became the first Brown women's team to win an Ivy title, taking the championship at the 1978 Outdoor Heptagonal meet.

Brown also enjoyed enormous early success in women's soccer, which had its first varsity season in 1975 and became an Ivy sport in 1978. The team won the Ivy tournament in 1980 to capture its first Ivy title. When round-robin play began in 1982, Brown went on to take the next nine Ivy titles and 10 of the first 11 championships. Between 1983 and 1990, Brown was nearly unbeatable in Ivy play, losing only once in 47 contests, including a 27-game unbeaten streak.

Brown was a pioneer in women's ice hockey, establishing the first collegiate women's ice hockey program in the country in 1964. The team had to travel to Canada during the early days in order to find competition. Women's ice hockey did not become an Ivy sport until the 1975–1976 season. Brown captured its first Ivy League championship during the 1980–1981 season and followed that up with Ivy titles in 1984–1985 and 1985–1986.

Women's basketball began intercollegiate competition during the 1973–1974 season and posted a 40-12 mark during its first three seasons. In 1974–1975, women's basketball became an Ivy League sport, and Brown tied for second in the Ivy League tournament. Brown finished second again the next year but went on to capture consecutive titles during the 1983–1984 and 1984–1985 seasons with the help of Ivy League Players of the Year Donna Yaffe '85 and Michelle Smith '86.

The women's swimming and diving team included two of Brown's most accomplished athletes, Noel Keefer '78 and Elaine Palmer '84. Keefer, a diver, was Brown's first female All-American, and Palmer won national championships in the 100 and 200 backstroke in 1982. Swimming did not become an Ivy sport until 1977, and from 1982 to 1985, Brown posted a perfect 18-0 slate and won three straight Ivy titles.

Another significant change occurred in 1988, when the athletic teams that had been called the Bruins for more than 50 years were now referred to as the Bears. Athletic director John Parry felt that "given our mascot was specifically a Brown Bear, I believed [the] use of bear was a clearer reference to our mascot than bruin." While the *Brown Daily Herald* continued to use Bruins and the *Providence Journal* used both terms, all official athletic department press releases now used Bears. Following the switch, Parry surveyed alumni and students through his column in the *Brown Sports* newsletter. While the alumni were slightly in favor of Bears, the students preferred Bruins by a 3-1 margin. Nonetheless, the change was made.

In his final collegiate game, Russ Tyler '71 poured in 46 points against the University of Rhode Island, just two points shy of the Brown single-game record. He sank six of his first seven shots on his way to 24 first-half points. In the second half, Tyler stayed hot but lost one basket when a foul was called on a teammate just before he shot. Late in the game, Brown coach Gerry Alaimo called a time-out to let his team know that Tyler was closing in on the record, but by then, there was little time left. Tyler tossed in a shot at the buzzer to finish with 46 points. With the crowd on its feet and applauding, his teammates picked him up and carried him off the court. Tyler finished with 568 points for the season, a new Brown record, and 1,133 points for his career, the fourth highest total at the time. He set the Brown records for assists in a season and a career and was second in the nation in free throw percentage (.871) as a senior.

Nancy Fuld '76 captained the tennis team and posted a 44-6 career mark. She set Brown records for wins in a season and a career. Fuld was nearly unbeatable during her final two years on College Hill with a 14-2 record as a junior and a 14-1 mark as a senior. She also played basketball at Brown and finished second on the team in scoring as a senior.

Noel Keefer '78 earned All-America honors in the three-meter dive at the 1975 Association for Intercollegiate Athletics for Women (AIAW) National Swimming and Diving Championships. Although she was only a freshman, she became the first woman in Brown history to be named an All-American. Keefer battled injuries throughout her career and spent the fall of her junior year in a body cast. After a grueling rehabilitation program, she returned to competition. Keefer went undefeated as a senior and won the New England championships.

Dom Starsia '74 was an All-American defenseman in 1973 and 1974. He also earned first-team All-Ivy and All-New England honors in both of these seasons. He returned to coach at Brown from 1983 to 1992 and guided his teams to two Ivy titles and five NCAA playoff appearances. He was named the NCAA Division I Coach of the Year in 1985 and 1991.

Tyler Chase '73 was the hero against the University of Pennsylvania in 1972, when he kicked five field goals to lift Brown to a 28-20 victory. He was a first-team All-Ivy selection and set the record for the longest field goal in Brown history with a 46-yard boot against Princeton. Chase was also a first-team All-Ivy golfer.

Arnie Berman '72 set the Brown career scoring mark with 1,668 points. As a senior, he poured in 38 points against Columbia and then matched that feat the following night with 38 points against Cornell. Berman led all New England scorers and finished 10th nationally with a 25.3 points-per-game scoring average during the 1971–1972 season. He was a first-team All-Ivy selection as a senior and was drafted in the fifth round by the NBA's Buffalo Braves.

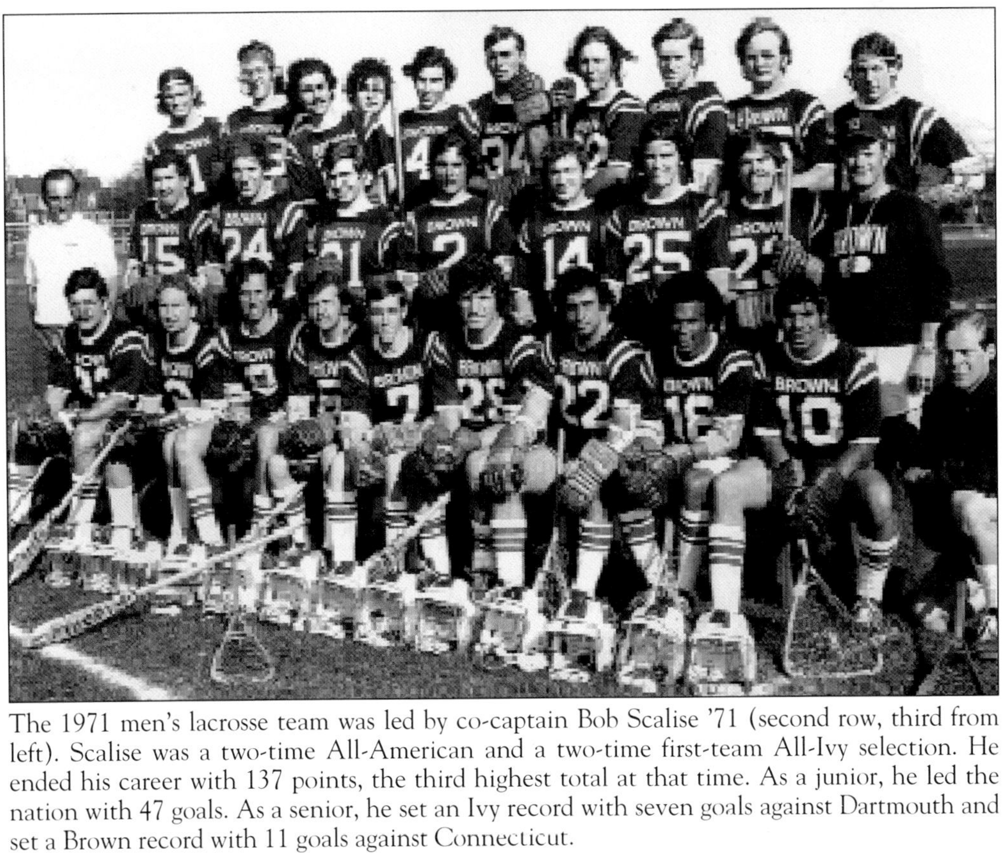

The 1971 men's lacrosse team was led by co-captain Bob Scalise '71 (second row, third from left). Scalise was a two-time All-American and a two-time first-team All-Ivy selection. He ended his career with 137 points, the third highest total at that time. As a junior, he led the nation with 47 goals. As a senior, he set an Ivy record with seven goals against Dartmouth and set a Brown record with 11 goals against Connecticut.

Anne Sullivan '81 won the 3,000-meter run and the 5,000-meter run at the 1979 Outdoor Heptagonal Championship and was a three-time first-team All-Ivy selection in cross country. She finished 18th at the AIAW national championship in cross country in 1979. In April 1980, she was featured in *Sports Illustrated* after setting an American women's record in the Cherry Blossom 10-mile run in Washington, D.C. Her time of 55:34 was 8 seconds better than the mark set by Joan Benoit a year earlier. Sullivan set an unofficial world record in the half marathon with a 1:13.13 clocking in the New Bedford race, breaking the previous record of 1:14.03. She placed fourth in the 10,000-meter run at the U.S. Olympic Trials in 1980 and ran in the marathon at the 1984 U.S. Olympic Trials. At the Boston Marathon in 1984, Sullivan was the first American woman to finish, completing the grueling course in 2:37.11.

Phil Brown '75 was a first-team All-Ivy and All-New England pick in 1974 and 1975 and once pulled down 24 rebounds in a game against Dartmouth. He set the Brown record with 931 career rebounds, and his 1,241 career points were the fifth highest total at the time.

The 1974–1975 varsity wrestling team included Lincoln Chafee '75 (bottom row, second from the right), who went on to become a senator from Rhode Island.

Bill Gilligan '77 was an All-Ivy and All-America selection in 1976. That year, he set Brown hockey records for assists in a season and points in a season while leading the Bruins to the Ivy title and a third-place finish in the NCAA tournament. Gilligan graduated as Brown's career leader in assists and points.

Bob McIntosh '77 was a first-team All-Ivy forward who teamed with Bill Gilligan '77 to lead Brown to the 1976 Ivy League championship and a third-place showing at the NCAA tournament. McIntosh tallied 81 goals and 160 points in his career, the second highest totals at the time.

Before Chris Berman '77 became a nationally known ESPN sports anchor, he got his start as the sports director for WBRU radio and the commentator for Brown basketball, football, and ice hockey games. In addition, Berman was a writer for the *Brown Daily Herald*.

Billy Almon '75 left Brown with 13 of 19 game, season, and career records. He was named the *Sporting News* College Baseball Player of the Year in 1974 and was the No. 1 pick in 1974 Major League Baseball draft by the San Diego Padres. He played 14 seasons in the majors with six different clubs and collected 842 hits, 128 stolen bases, and a .255 batting average. His best season came in 1981, when he hit .301 for Chicago.

Steve Ralbovsky '76 was a first-team All-Ivy and All-America pick in 1974 and 1975. He was named the Outstanding Defensive Player in the 1975 NCAA tournament and won the Robert R. Hermann Trophy in 1975 as the top college player. Ralbovsky was the first player selected in the 1976 college soccer draft by both professional soccer leagues and played for the U.S. national team in 1977 and 1978.

Fred Pereira '77 was a first-team All-American in 1974 and 1976 and a second-team All-American in 1975. A three-time first-team All-Ivy and All-New England selection, he graduated with every season and career scoring record in soccer in Brown history. He led his teams to three consecutive Ivy titles and NCAA appearances, including a third-place finish in 1975. Pereira was the second player selected in the North American Soccer League draft.

Peter Moss '80 was a two-time first-team All-Ivy selection and the Ivy League Player of the Year in 1980. He led the Ivy League in scoring as a senior, and when he graduated, his 1,241 career points were the fifth highest total in Brown history. As a senior, he scored 38 points against Harvard to lead Brown to an 85-76 triumph.

The men's crew varsity eight captured the IRA championship for the first time in 1979. The crew included, from left to right, Peter LeViness '80, Charles Riedel '79, Bill Scholtz '79, Vaughn Gangwish '79, and coxswain Norm Alpert '80.

Brian Saunders '77 was a two-time first-team All-Ivy pick and left Brown with 1,288 points, the fourth highest total at the time. He also set the Brown records for field goals in a season and a career. Saunders was the team captain as a junior and a senior and led the Ivy League in scoring in both seasons. As a senior, he scored 39 points to lead Brown to a 91-83 victory over Columbia.

Trish Wurtz '82 became the first Brown woman to score 1,000 points. She was a four-time All-Ivy selection and earned a spot on the first team in 1980. Wurtz also set the Brown record for career rebounds with 916.

Amy Crafts '82 was the first women's ice hockey player in Ivy League history to be named first-team All-Ivy four times and was the Ivy League Player of the Year in 1981. She graduated with the Brown records for goals, assists, and points in a career. Crafts also set Brown records for goals in a game (five), assists in a game (five), and points in a game (seven).

Steve Jordan '82 was a two-time first-team All-Ivy selection and an Associated Press honorable mention All-America pick in 1980. He set Brown records for most receiving yards in a game and a season. He played 13 seasons in the NFL with the Minnesota Vikings and was a six-time All-Pro, earning a spot on the squad every year from 1986 to 1991.

Linebacker John Woodring '81 was a first-team All-Ivy pick in 1979 and 1980 and an Associated Press honorable mention All-American in 1980. He led the team in tackles in each of his three years and finished with 313 career tackles. Woodring was taken in the sixth round of the 1981 NFL draft by the New York Jets and went on to play five seasons with them.

Frances Fusco '83 was a four-time first-team All-Ivy selection and a two-time All-American. She set the Brown record with 20 career assists. When she graduated, Fusco was third in career goals (28) and third in career points (76).

The 1984 women's soccer team was ranked No. 1 in the country for two weeks and finished the season ranked second nationally. The team posted 12 shutouts in 15 games and allowed only three goals all season, outscoring its opponents 38-3. Coach Phil Pincince's squad went 13-1-1 overall, including a perfect 6-0 mark in Ivy play. The team advanced to the NCAA quarterfinals but dropped a 1-0 decision to the University of Connecticut.

Debbie Fuhrman '84 was the Ivy League vault champion in 1982, 1983, and 1984. She finished first in the floor exercise at the 1982 NCAA regionals and placed sixth in the floor exercise at the 1982 NCAA championship.

Jon Smith '83 (fourth from the left) was a member of the Brown varsity eight that won the IRA championship in 1983. He won the silver medal at the 1984 Olympics in the U.S. coxless four and the bronze medal at the 1988 Olympics in the U.S. eight.

Gretchen Orr '85 was a two-time first-team All-Ivy and All-New England pick. She was the Ivy League Player of the Year in 1983 and an All-America selection in 1984. Her teams won three Ivy titles and made three NCAA tournament appearances.

Teresa Abrahamsohn '85 was a two-time first-team All-Ivy selection and the Ivy League Player of the Year in 1984. She was a first-team All-New England and All-America pick in 1984, and her soccer teams won three Ivy titles and made three NCAA tournament appearances. Abrahamsohn was also a first-team All-Ivy softball player.

Kevin Tracy '85 was a two-time first-team All-Ivy golfer. He tied for second at the 1985 Ivy League tournament to record the highest finish ever for a Brown golfer. Tracy also placed fourth at the 1982 Ivy League tournament.

Elaine Palmer '84 was the 1982 AIAW national champion in the 100-yard backstroke and the 200-yard backstroke. When she graduated, she held eight individual school records and was a member of four record-setting relay teams. She won eight individual Ivy crowns and four Eastern titles. Palmer was an All-American in three of four seasons and qualified for the U.S. Olympic Trials in 1980 and 1984.

Mardie Corcoran '86 was the Ivy League Player of the Year and the Eastern Collegiate Athletic Conference (ECAC) Player of the Year in 1985 and 1986. In only 80 career games, she scored 100 goals and dished out 105 assists. She set Brown career records for goals, assists, and points. An outstanding all-around athlete, she was also a first-team All-Ivy softball player.

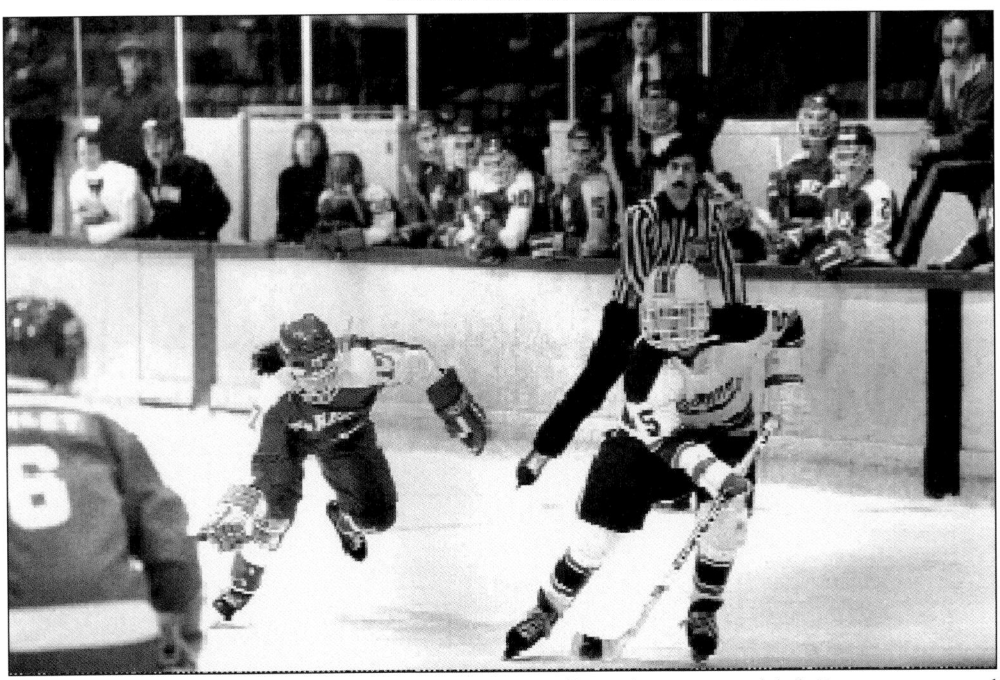

Lisa Bishop '86 (right) was a two-time first-team All-Ivy honoree and left Brown in second place in career goals (98), assists (89), and points (187). She finished second in the Ivy League in scoring as a junior and led the league in scoring as a senior. Bishop combined with Mardie Corcoran '86 to lead Brown to Ivy titles in 1984–1985 and 1985–1986.

Jim Turner '86 was the Ivy League Player of the Year in 1986 and helped lead Brown to the Ivy title and an NCAA tournament appearance. Turner set Brown records for field-goal percentage in a game, a season, and a career. Turner made 14 of 15 shots in a game against Pennsylvania in 1986 for a remarkable .933 field-goal percentage. He shot 62.8 percent during his senior year and connected on 60.2 percent of his shots in his career.

Tom Gagnon '86 was the Ivy League Rookie of the Year in 1983 and the Ivy League Player of the Year in 1986. He was a three-time All-American and graduated as the program's all-time leading scorer with 109 goals and 99 assists for 208 career points.

Donna Yaffe '85 was the Ivy League Rookie of the Year in 1982 and a two-time Ivy League Player of the Year. A three-time All-American and a three-time first-team All-Ivy selection, Yaffe tied the Brown record for points in a game with 37 points against Westfield State. She set the Brown record for points in a season and graduated as the program's all-time leading scorer with 1,779 points.

Colleen O'Day '86 was a four-time first-team All-Ivy selection and the Ivy League Player of the Year in 1985. She was also a two-time All-American. Her teams won four consecutive Ivy titles and played in four NCAA tournaments.

Bob Hill '88 was a two-time Ivy League Wrestler of the Year and Brown's first Eastern Intercollegiate Wrestling Association (EIWA) champion in 1987 and 1988. He set the Brown records for dual-meet wins in a season with 19 and dual-meet wins in a career with 61. Hill also set the Brown mark for most dual-meet points in a season with 79 points as a sophomore and then broke his own record the following season with 89 points.

Patrick Lynch '87 helped the Bruins to the 1986 Ivy title and an NCAA tournament appearance. He was a tri-captain as a senior and finished as the second leading scorer in the Ivy League with a 21.5 points-per-game average. Lynch turned in two of the top scoring performances in Marvel Gym history when he poured in 42 points against Dartmouth and scored 39 points versus Yale. He was elected Rhode Island attorney general in 2002.

Lauren Becker '87 was a two-time first-team All-Ivy lacrosse player. She was the Ivy League Rookie of the Year in 1984 and the Ivy League Player of the Year in 1987. Becker set Brown marks for assists in a season and a career and points in a season and a career. She also registered at least one point in 40 consecutive games to set a Brown record. In field hockey, Becker was a three-time first-team All-Ivy pick.

Tim Donovan '89 was named the Player of the Year in the Eastern Intercollegiate Tennis Association (EITA) in 1988 and 1989. He was selected to the EITA first team in singles in each of his four seasons and competed in singles at three NCAA championships. Donovan compiled a career 48-8 singles record in dual-meet action, including a perfect 14-0 mark as a junior. He was ranked 54th in the country at the end of his senior year and went on to compete professionally in the U.S. Open, the French Open, and the Australian Open.

Greg Whiteley '89 became the first Brown runner to win an NCAA championship when he won the 3,000-meter run at the 1989 NCAA Indoor Track and Field Championships. He won eight Heptagonal titles during his Brown career and was a six-time All-American. Whiteley became the first Brown runner to break a four-minute mile when he posted a time of 3:59.15 at the Jackie Joyner Invitational in Los Angeles.

Theresa Hirschauer '89 was a four-time first-team All-Ivy selection, the 1985 Ivy League Rookie of the Year, and the 1988 Ivy League Player of the Year. A two-time All-American, she set the Brown and Ivy League records for goals in a season and a career and points in a season and a career. Hirschauer also played softball and was a three-time first-team All-Ivy pick.

Six

National and International Success 1990–2003

While Brown had enjoyed some success in the Ivy League and against regional competition, the 1990s saw the rise of Brown athletes and teams on the national and international stage.

The Brown crew programs set the tone with seven national titles during this period. The men's crew dominated in the mid-1990s with national titles in 1993, 1994, and 1995. Women's crew followed with a national championship in 1996 and Brown's first NCAA team title in any sport in 1999. The women also won NCAA titles in 2000 and 2002. Both the men's and women's programs had international success with victories at the prestigious Royal Henley Regatta in England.

The women's ice hockey team has been a perennial national power and played in the NCAA championship game during the 2001–2002 season. The men's lacrosse team, which has consistently been ranked among the top teams in the country, advanced to the NCAA semifinals in 1994. The men's basketball team capped off a record-breaking season in 2003 by earning its first-ever at-large bid to the National Invitation Tournament (NIT).

Besides the tremendous team accomplishments, individual athletes have also been honored as national players of the year. Lacrosse attackman Darren Lowe '92 won the Lt. Raymond Enners Memorial Award in 1992 as the Division I Player of the Year. Devon Kennedy '99 won the 1999 Betty Richey Award as the outstanding senior squash player in the nation, and Ali Brewer '00 won the 2000 Patty Kazmaier Award as the national women's ice hockey player of the year.

Brown athletes have also demonstrated excellence in international competition. Between 1996 and 2002, Brown athletes won as many gold medals (four) as they had during the previous 100 years. In fact, each of Brown's gold medalists during this period—Xeno Muller, Becky Kellar, Katie King, and Tara Mounsey—also won silver medals at a different Olympics.

The entire athletic program was recognized in 2002 by *U.S. News and World Report* as one of the top 20 athletic programs in the country out of 321 Division I schools. The selection was based on several factors, including gender equity, win-loss record, number of sports offered, and graduation rate.

With the university's lofty reputation as one of America's best athletic programs, it would seem that this level of achievement will continue for many more years.

Michael Brewer '92 was the Ivy League Player of the Year and a first-team All-American in 1992. Brewer was selected to play on the Canadian national team in the 1991 USA Cup Tournament and was drafted by the NHL's Washington Capitals.

Carolyn Thornton '90 was a two-time first-team All-Ivy outfielder and helped the 1990 softball squad to the Ivy title and a school-record 31 wins. She became the first full-time female sports writer at the *Providence Journal* in 1986 and was named the Rhode Island Sports Writer of the Year by the National Sportscasters and Sportswriters Association in 1998.

Suzanne Bailey '91 was the Ivy League Rookie of the Year in 1987 and the Ivy League Player of the Year in 1990. A four-time first-team All-Ivy selection, her soccer teams won four Ivy League titles and compiled a dominating 22-1-1 mark against Ivy competition. In addition, Bailey earned All-America honors in 1990. Bailey also played lacrosse and was a two-time first-team All-Ivy pick and the Ivy League Player of the Year in 1991. She was a two-time All-American in lacrosse and graduated with the Brown records for goals in a season and a career.

Darren Lowe '92 graduated as the second leading scorer in NCAA Division I history with 316 points. The 1992 U.S. Intercollegiate Lacrosse Association Division I Player of the Year and Attackman of the Year, Lowe was a three-time All-American and set the Brown career records for assists and points. The Ivy League Rookie of the Year in 1989 and the Ivy League Player of the Year in 1992, he was a three-time first-team All-Ivy pick and set the Ivy League record for career points.

Christy Trexler '93 was the Ivy League Rookie of the Year in 1990 and a two-time first-team All-Ivy pick. She set Brown softball career records for wins, winning percentage, strikeouts, and earned run average.

Susan Smith '93 won 15 individual Heptagonal titles during her Brown career, including four consecutive titles in the 100-meter hurdles and the 400-meter hurdles. She was named the Outstanding Performer at the 1992 Indoor Heptagonal Championship after winning the 55-meter dash, the 55-meter hurdles, and anchoring the winning one-mile relay team. Smith competed for Ireland in the 1996 Summer Olympics in Atlanta and also placed seventh in the 400-meter hurdles at the 1997 World Track and Field Championships.

Eileen Rocchio '93 was the Ivy League All-Around champion in 1990 and won Ivy titles in the vault in 1990 and 1991 and the floor exercises in 1991. She qualified for the NCAA regionals in 1992 and 1993.

Christine Monteiro '93 was a three-time first-team All-Ivy selection and an All-America choice as a senior. She set the Brown records for goals in a career and points in a career.

Scott Hanley '93 was a first-team All-Ivy forward who helped Brown to the 1991 Ivy championship and a spot in the 1993 NCAA tournament. Hanley led the Bears in scoring as a senior and finished with 59 career goals, the eighth best total at the time.

Derek Chauvette '93 was an excellent playmaker and a first-team All-Ivy center. He amassed 99 career assists and graduated second all-time in that category. He teamed with Scott Hanley '93 to lead the Bears to the Ivy title in 1991 and the NCAA tournament in 1993. Chauvette led the Ivy League in scoring as a junior with 22 points in 10 games.

Jamie Koven '95 was part of the Brown varsity eight that won three consecutive National Collegiate Rowing Championships and IRA titles. He won a gold medal with the U.S. eight at the 1994 World Championship and won the 1997 World Championship in single sculls, becoming the first American sculler to win in 30 years. Koven was a member of the U.S. eight at the 1996 Olympics and rowed in the U.S. straight four in the 2000 Olympics.

Andy Towers '93 was a three-time All-American and became the first Brown player to earn first-team All-America honors twice. The 1993 Ivy League Player of the Year, Towers set the Brown record with 150 career goals. As a sophomore, he set the Brown single-season record with 59 goals. When he graduated, Towers became just the third player in Brown history to top 200 career points, finishing with 203 points.

Todd Carey '93 earned All-Eastern Intercollegiate Baseball League honors in each of his three seasons before being drafted by the Boston Red Sox in 1992. He played professional baseball for nine seasons, including three seasons in Triple A.
Carey was an All-Star in 1996 with the Trenton Thunder, the AA affiliate of the Boston Red Sox. He set Brown records for runs scored in a season and assists in a season and tied the Brown record with four stolen bases in a game against URI.

Darren Eales '95 was a three-time first-team All-Ivy pick and a first-team All-American in 1994. He was selected the national At-Large Academic All-American of the Year in the spring of 1995. When he graduated, his 31 career goals ranked sixth, and his 83 career points ranked fourth in Brown history. Eales tied the Brown record by scoring a goal in nine consecutive games, and set the Brown record by registering a point in 12 consecutive games.

Mia Dammen '95 was a first-team All-Ivy honoree in 1992 and finished her Brown career in fifth place in goals scored (29), second in career assists (29), and third in career points (87). As a senior, she helped lead Brown to the Ivy title and the quarterfinals of the NCAA tournament.

Allison Schettini '98 was a first-team All-Ivy honoree and a third-team All-America selection in 1997. She tallied 107 goals and 50 assists to finish second all-time in scoring at Brown with 157 career points.

Martina Jerant '95 was the Ivy League Rookie of the Year in 1992 and the Ivy League Player of the Year in 1993. A three-time first-team All-Ivy selection, she led her teams to three consecutive Ivy titles and an NCAA tournament appearance in 1994. She graduated as the second leading scorer in Brown history while setting the record for career rebounds. Jerant played for Canada in the 1996 Olympics and played professionally in Croatia.

Cathy Luke '95 was a two-time first-team All-Ivy choice and the Ivy League Player of the Year in 1994. She set a Brown record with 34 digs in a match against Harvard and graduated with the Brown record for hitting percentage in a career.

Kerri Whitaker '96 was a first-team All-Ivy and All-America selection in lacrosse in 1996 and was a member of the U.S. women's lacrosse squad in 1996, 1997 and 1998. She was also a first-team All-Ivy pick in field hockey as a senior. Whitaker posted career totals of 85 goals and 34 assists in lacrosse and graduated fifth all-time in scoring with 119 points.

David Evans '96 was a two-time USILA first-team All-American. He was the 1993 Ivy League Rookie of the Year and the 1995 Ivy League Player of the Year. When he graduated, his 145 career goals and 232 career points both ranked second all-time at Brown. Evans was also a first-team All-Ivy and All-New England pick in 1994 and 1995.

Ryan Mulhern '96 was the Ivy League Rookie of the Year in 1993 and the Ivy League Player of the Year in 1995. His 61 career goals were the eighth best total in Brown history at the time. Mulhern tied the Brown record for game-winning goals in a season with five and went on to play in the NHL for the Washington Capitals.

Xeno Muller '95 won a gold medal for Switzerland in the single sculls at the 1996 Olympics in Atlanta and a silver medal at the 2000 Olympics in Sydney. Muller was part of the 1993 Brown varsity eight, which went undefeated and won the Eastern Sprints, IRA regatta, and the National Collegiate Rowing Championship.

Becky Kellar '97 won a gold medal at the 2002 Olympics in Salt Lake City and a silver medal at the 1998 Olympics in Nagano as a member of the Canadian women's ice hockey team. She was a three-time All-Ivy pick in ice hockey and finished sixth in career scoring at Brown. Kellar also played softball at Brown and was a two-time first-team All-Ivy selection. She set Brown softball records for hits in a season and a career.

Greg Cattrano '97 was the U.S. Intercollegiate Lacrosse Association Goalie of the Year, a first-team All-American, and a first-team All-Ivy pick in 1997. His three career goals set an NCAA record for a goalie. Cattrano was also a second-team All-American in 1996.

Katie King '97 won a gold medal at the 1998 Winter Olympics in Nagano and a silver medal at the 2002 Winter Olympics in Salt Lake City as a member of the U.S. women's ice hockey team. Brown's all-time leading scorer in ice hockey, King was a three-time first-team All-Ivy and All-ECAC pick. A three-time Ivy League Player of the Year and the 1997 ECAC Player of the Year, she set Brown records for most goals in a season and in a career, as well as most points in a season and in a career. King also played softball at Brown and was the 1996 Ivy League Player of the Year and the 1997 Ivy League Pitcher of the Year. As a senior, she almost single-handedly led Brown to the Ivy title and its first NCAA tournament appearance. While King was finishing up hockey season, the softball squad struggled to a 2-13-1 record, but when she returned, the Bears won 18 of their final 26 regular season games. In her first game with the team, King tossed a two-hit shutout and went 3-3 at the plate.

Danielle Solari '97 earned All-Ivy honors in each of her four years, including a spot on the first team as a sophomore. She closed out her career in fourth place all-time in goals, third in assists, and fourth in points. Solari also set a Brown single-season record with 44 assists during the 1996–1997 campaign.

Helen Betancourt '98 helped lead Brown to two Ivy and Eastern Sprints titles and the 1996 National Collegiate Rowing Championship. She was a member of four national teams from 1997 through 2000 and was an alternate in the U.S. eight at the 2000 Olympics in Sydney.

Tivon Abel '98 was a three-time first-team All-Ivy pick and a two-time EIWA champion. He finished fifth at the 1998 NCAA tournament to earn All-America honors.

Porter Collins '98 (left) and Ben Holbrook '97 (right) were oarsmen on the 1995 Brown varsity eight that won the national championship. The two men also rowed in the U.S. coxed four and won a gold medal at the 1995 World Championship. In addition, Collins competed in the U.S. eight at the 1996 Olympics in Atlanta and the 2000 Olympics in Sydney.

Liz Turner '98 was a two-time first-team All-Ivy selection and became the first player in Ivy League basketball history—men's and women's—to amass 1,000 points, 500 rebounds, 250 assists, 150 steals, and 100 three-pointers in a career. In the Brown record book, she ranked in the top 10 in 14 different statistical categories when she graduated. Her legacy at Brown was assured when Liz and Kim Chace donated $1.4 million to endow the women's basketball head-coaching position. The unique aspect of the gift was that it was named for Turner, who was a junior captain of the team at the time. The Liz Turner '98 Coaching Chair was only the second such position in the country to be completely endowed.

Ali Brewer '00 won the 2000 Patty Kazmaier Award as the national women's ice hockey player of the year. She was also the Ivy League Player of the Year and the ECAC Goaltender of the Year. Brewer's teams made three consecutive trips to the American Women's College Hockey Alliance (AWCHA) national semifinals, including two appearances in the national championship game.

Women's crew captured Brown's first NCAA team title in any sport in 1999. The Bears defeated Virginia by three seconds in the varsity eight grand final to win the team title. Pictured, from left to right, are the following: (front row) Caroline Grogan '00, Erin Kelley '02, Kate Saul '00, Amy Meyers '99, and Nina Carter '00; (back row) coach John Murphy, Kellie Walker '00, Anda Adams '00, Portia Johnson '01, and Rachel Anderson '00.

Vita Redding '99 graduated as Brown's all-time leading scorer with 1,962 points. Redding earned All-Ivy recognition in each of her four seasons, including first-team honors in 1997 and 1999. As a sophomore, she ranked fifth in the country in scoring with a 23.8 points-per-game average. Redding became the first Brown player to score at least 400 points in each of her four seasons, and she graduated with nine Brown records.

[illegible] '[illegible] was the Ivy League Rookie of the Year in [illegible]98 and the Ivy League Player of the Year in 2001. She graduated with 4,026 career assists, eclipsing the previous Brown record by more than [illegible]400 assists.

Tomo Nakanishi '00 became only the fourth player in Ivy League history to earn first-team All-Ivy honors for four years. She was named the Ivy League Rookie of the Year in 1996 and the Ivy League Player of the Year in 1998. Nakanishi's teams won two Ivy titles and made two NCAA tournament appearances.

Trinity Gray '00 was the national runner-up in the 800-meter run at the 1999 NCAA Indoor Track and Field Championships. He was selected as the U.S. Track Coaches Association (USTCA) Regional Indoor Athlete of the Year in 2000 and was named the Outstanding Performer at the 2000 Indoor Track and Field Heptagonal Championships.

Sean Morey '99 was the 1995 Ivy League Rookie of the Year and the 1997 Ivy League Player of the Year. He was a three-time first-team All-Ivy pick. A second-team Associated Press All-American in 1997 and a second-team ESPN-*USA Today* All-American in 1998, Morey set 5 Ivy League and 11 Brown records. He ranked third all-time in NCAA I-AA history in career receptions and career receiving yards. He played professional football for the New England Patriots, Philadelphia Eagles, and Barcelona Dragons.

Devon Kennedy '99 won the 1999 Betty Richey Award as the outstanding senior squash player in the nation. She was a four-time first-team All-America selection and finished second at the 1999 Women's Intercollegiate Squash Racquets Association championship.

James Perry '00 was the 1999 Ivy League Player of the Year and the winner of the George Bulger Lowe Award as the Best Offensive Player in New England. He was a three-time first-team All-Ivy selection and graduated with 10 Ivy League and 17 Brown passing records. Perry finished his career as the 17th most prolific passer in NCAA I-AA history with 9,294 career passing yards.

Cory Gibbs '01 was a three-time first-team All-Ivy selection and the Ivy League Player of the Year as a senior. Gibbs went on to play professionally for FC St. Pauli in the German Bundesliga and became the youngest American to score a goal in the German first division. Gibbs also made the U.S. national team and earned his first cap in 2003 in a match against New Zealand.

Caroline Grogan '00 (left) and Kate Saul '00 (right) celebrate immediately after winning a second consecutive NCAA title in the varsity eight in 2000. Grogan and Saul also won an NCAA crown in 1997 in the varsity four and captured three consecutive Ivy and Eastern Sprints titles in their three years in the Brown varsity eight.

All-American Chas Gessner '03 tied an NCAA I-AA record with 24 receptions in a game against the University of Rhode Island. Gessner caught 114 passes during the 2002 season, which ranked third in I-AA history. He was the 1999 Ivy League Rookie of the Year and a two-time first-team All-Ivy pick. As a senior, he led the nation with 11.4 receptions per game.

Tara Mounsey '01 won the gold medal at 1998 Winter Olympics and the silver medal at the 2002 Winter Olympics. She was a three-time first-team All-Ivy and All-ECAC selection in ice hockey. Mounsey also played field hockey at Brown and was a 1999 All-America selection and the Ivy League Player of the Year. She set Brown records for goals and points in a season and a career in field hockey.

Stephen Campbell '01 set an NCAA I-AA single-season record with 120 receptions as a senior. He was an Associated Press first-team All-American and won the George Bulger Lowe Award as the New England Player of the Year. Campbell was a three-time first-team All-Ivy selection and amassed 305 career receptions, the second best total in NCAA I-AA history at the time.

Corre Myer '02 was the Ivy League Rookie of the Year in 1998 and the Ivy League Player of the Year in 2001. She graduated with 4,026 career assists, eclipsing the previous Brown record by more than 1,400 assists.

Earl Hunt '03 became the first Brown player and just the fourth Ivy League player to score 2,000 points, finishing with 2,041 career points. He was also the second Brown player and only the 23rd Ivy League player to be named first-team All-Ivy three times. Hunt's 39 points against Harvard set a Pizzitola Center single-game scoring record.

Mike Malan '02 set the Brown records for rushing in a game (267 yards), a season (1,213 yards), and a career (3,266). He was a two-time first-team All-Ivy selection and an honorable mention All-American as a senior. At the time of his graduation, his 3,266 career rushing yards ranked fifth best in Ivy League history, while his 39 career touchdowns were fourth in the Ivy record book.